# Powerful Affirmations to Reprogram Your Subconscious Mind

## *Your Amazing Itty Bitty Affirmations Book - 15 Ways to Make Positive Messages Work for You*

Your negative limiting beliefs and subconscious programming, derived from childhood, shape and rule your adult life – your decisions, your experiences and your emotional wellbeing.

In this practical Itty Bitty Book, Micaela Passeri, shows you a step by step process on how to create and craft powerful, custom affirmations, unique to you as an individual that will reprogram your subconscious mind by turning off your negative thought patterns replacing them with more empowering ones.

You will learn how to:

- Identify which subconscious negative beliefs are disempowering you.

- Identify the structure in which to write affirmations that will reprogram your mind to the positive.

- Write powerful affirmations that get results.

**Pick up a copy of this powerful book today and experience the permanent benefits of positive thinking and affirmations in all areas of your life: Financial, Relationships, Health, Emotional and Spiritual.**

# Your Amazing
# Itty Bitty®
# Affirmations
# Book

*15 Ways to Make Empowering Messages*
*Work for You*

## Micaela Passeri

Published by Itty Bitty® Publishing
A subsidiary of S&P Productions, Inc.

Printed in the United States of America

Itty Bitty® Publishing
311 Main Street, Suite D
El Segundo, CA 90245
(310) 640-8885


ISBN: 978-1-931191-72-2

*To my loving, kind, compassionate, smart, beautiful and talented daughter, you are my inspiration every day. All I do is for you. I love you so much!*

*To my mom, for all you have done and do for Arabella and me; truly I could not have done it without you. Knowing I have you in my corner has given me the strength to keep going. I love you.*

*To my father, who is no longer with us, he would have been so excited to know I wrote a book! I have so much of him in me, his entrepreneurial spirit, his fire, his passion, his ability to dream and live in possibility. Thank you for all the lessons, the hard ones and the easy ones. I know you are watching over and smiling down. I miss you very much!*

Stop by our Itty Bitty® Publishing website to read many more interesting articles about affirmations:

www.ittybittypublishing.com

Or visit Micaela at

www.LoveYouRevolution.com/gift

Enjoy!

# Table of Contents

Introduction

# Introduction

Affirmations.......Do they work? Can they really help?

Well, they are a debated issue. Some say they are useless and others say they really work! So who do we believe?

The purpose of an affirmation is to send a message from your conscious mind to your subconscious mind so that your subconscious mind takes the message as truth, because the sole duty of your subconscious mind is to manifest that which it thinks is truth.

In a perfect world, you would want to fill your subconscious mind with beneficial habits you want to manifest through affirmations. However, we are humans with free will, intellect, beliefs, conditioning, emotions and feelings, which all contribute to the distortion, manipulation and interpretation of any message the conscious mind relays to the subconscious mind. This is what makes it harder for affirmations to be fully effective. In this Itty Bitty® book you will learn how to bypass all these "message interrupters" so your affirmations can be powerful and have the positive and shifting effect they are intended to have.

Affirmations have been used for centuries by powerful people who swear by them, yet many other people use them and feel they don't work. So what do the powerful people know that other people don't? What has some people so ecstatic about the effects of affirmations and others yell blasphemy? The difference is the way in which the successful people write the affirmations and what they are written about, and how connected that person is with their affirmations.

Get ready to embark on a fun and creative journey that will show you how you can write effective affirmations and have them bring huge rewards in your life!

<u>First Tip:</u> You will be focusing on positive affirmations. Since affirmations can be positive and negative and since they are used in a repetitive manner, you want to make sure you are repeating the positive ones!

# Step 1
## Choose a Compelling Topic – Area of Life

Ready? Let's start! The first thing you must think about when creating your affirmations is: what topics do you want to write your affirmations about. Do you want to write affirmations around a goal? A way of being? Or do you want to write them to counteract a negative belief or pattern?

1. Start by listing the areas in your life you want to work on. In those areas what particular goal do you want to achieve positive results in?
2. Take inventory of your most positive abilities, qualities and traits. What is special about you? What is unique? What are you most proud of?
3. Write a list of negative beliefs you want to dispel. Negative perceptions can be disempowering in everything we do. With affirmations, one can change these harmful self-perceptions and turn them into empowering messages.
4. Write down emotional words that you connect with. This will help make the affirmations feel in alignment with who you are.

We are trained to see what we are not, instead of what we truly are. This is where affirmations come in; listing your positive qualities helps you feel confident in who you are, which then helps you write an effective affirmation to counteract the negative belief.

## Questions To Ask Yourself When Writing An Affirmation:

- What area in my life do I want to start working on?
- What qualities do I value in myself? This will help you stay in awareness and keep them in the forefront of your mind.
- Does this feel good to me?
- Can I relate to this affirmation?
- Do I feel disconnected when saying this affirmation?
- What is the result I want from using this affirmation?

## A Benefit of Affirmations

- Boost your self-esteem

# Step 2
## Prioritize Your Topics –
## What is Most Important Right Now

To make affirmations more effective, it is best to focus on a few at a time, especially if you are working with countering a negative belief (these are deep and ingrained, and sometimes harder to release). And it is best to work with ones that relate to the same topic.

If you are having a hard time picking topics, pick whichever area causes you most pain, anxiety or discomfort. Those are the ones that need your immediate attention. You want to be very clear and specific when communicating to the subconscious mind. Here is how you do it:

1.  Gauge which area of your life has the most pain or discomfort.
2.  Choose two or three topics within that area of life to work on. Focused attention gives faster results.
3.  Connect your topics with the goals you want to achieve. Doing this will help hone in on the intent of the affirmation. For example, if you are trying to quit smoking, courage, willpower and strength are things you might want to write your affirmation around.
4.  Update them as things improve and you feel results, so you can start working on new topics.

**Questions To Ask Yourself When Prioritizing:**

- Is this a topic I really need to work on right now or is there a more pressing area of life I need to focus on?
- Can I wait to work on the other topics?
- What is most important to me when thinking about this topic?
- How would I feel if I released this negative belief or achieved this goal?
- How long have I been struggling with this topic? Sometimes this is an indication that you need to tend to a particular goal/belief/area of life.

**A Benefit of Affirmations**

- Make you feel confident in who you are

# Step 3
## Affirmations Must Be Believable
## To The Subconscious Mind

Write your affirmations in the present tense; make it personal and positive. Affirmations are statements that speak about something in your life as if it has already happened. They need to be clear and bold in order to rattle old patterns and dissolve them. Some people say there's no problem in writing affirmations as "I can" or "I will" statements, but I believe that when you put something in the future, it doesn't feel real, while, when you say "I Am" or use the present tense, it has a different connotation to it.

1. Using an "I Am" statement helps the subconscious mind think what you are saying has already happened, thus putting in place all the mechanisms it needs to make it reality.
2. They must be personal because they must be believable to you in order for the subconscious to even consider it as true. Your conscious mind also has to feel in alignment or else it won't give the importance it needs to the affirmation.
3. The subconscious does not recognize negatives. "I don't want to be weak," will be heard as "I want to be weak." So it will give you more to feel weak about.
4. Instead, if you affirm courage and strength, then the subconscious will give you more of that.

5

## Questions to Ask Yourself Before You Write Your Affirmations

- What do I want to affirm?
- Do I connect to it?
- What will make it personal to me?
- How does it make me feel?
- Do I believe it?

## A Benefit of Affirmations

- Change your life for the better by helping you stay optimistic

# Step 4
## The Subconscious Mind Must Have Proof

Because we communicate with the subconscious mind through feelings and not words, the subconscious mind will believe when a feeling is associated with an action, and therefore it creates the proof that it needs to believe.

For example, most people who are in a poverty mindset associate the feeling of pain to money and it is that feeling that perpetuates the "lack" of money because one of the subconscious mind's jobs is to not make us "feel" pain.

Here are three easy ways to give the subconscious mind the proof it needs:

1. When you have the proof, state the affirmation (fastest way).
2. Embed the affirmation through repetition so it seems real – "fake it till you make it."
3. Trick, or better said – rewire your mind to believing there is proof (an exercise below will help).

The latter one is a bit tricky, no pun intended, but if you can trick the mind to thinking there is proof already, then the affirmation is just there to seal it in.

## Exercise for Rewiring the Mind

Using the example from above, if you are one of those people who associates money with pain, one thing you could do right when spending your money is saying an affirmation like "I always have more money to spend" and as long as you always have money left in your pocket, the subconscious mind will believe the affirmation to be true and slowly your poverty mindset will turn into an abundance mindset.

There are three things to keep in mind:

- Always check in with how you "feel" when you are rewiring the mind; remember the subconscious mind understands feelings, not words.
- You can apply this to any area of life just as long as you can show the subconscious mind the proof.
- Connecting to a positive feeling when rewiring is of utmost importance.

## A Benefit of Affirmations

- Rewire the brain to function in a more efficient and positive manner, thus resulting in more focused results

# Step 5
## Affirmations Must Spark a Feeling

As we have been talking about in the previous chapter, in order to really make affirmations work we need to have a positive feeling associated with the affirmation and the feeling must be believable to you.

You can trigger feelings in three different ways:

1. Using words that involve and invoke feelings is most commonly used when writing affirmations.
2. Using visualization is just as powerful, but used less frequently since not everyone is familiar with this concept. Imagining that you already have or you already experience what you are affirming is a great way to keep your affirmation in the forefront of your mind.
3. Using a tool called "acting as if" is also used less frequently and is unfamiliar to most people, but when you act as if what you want already exists, associating the feelings of already having that which you want (or the experience you want), the brain starts creating new pathways, thus affirming your affirmation.

## Example of "Acting As If"...

A friend of mine has been determined to be wealthy. She grew up in the projects and experienced what the lack of wealth felt like. As an adult woman she consciously started to do the following things to rewire her mind to think she already was wealthy:

- First, she surrounded herself with a beautiful home environment that was pleasing to her and made her feel wealthy.
- She wrote her wealth affirmations all over the place.
- She commissioned a painting to say "I Am Rich" on it.
- When speaking to people she always talked about how rich she was and all the things she was in the process of doing because of her wealth.
- She embodied the feelings, used the words and said the affirmations a wealthy person would.

Needless to say, her income went up, she started meeting and associating with wealthy people, she started traveling like a wealthy person – thanks to acting as if she is well on her way to being wealthy!

## A Benefit of Affirmations

- Make you feel good about yourself

## Step 6
### Affirmations Must Be Positive

Affirmations are useless if they contain any negative prepositions or construct. They must be written in the positive. The following are a few examples of what *not* to do, along with a respective positive counterpart:

1. "I stop gaining weight." Instead use "I lose 10 pounds by November 1st, 2017" or "I maintain my current weight starting October 30th, 2017."
2. "I accumulate fewer and fewer bills." Instead use "All my bills are paid on time by January 1st, 2017" or "I pay my bills in full every month."

As you can see, a negative affirmation can come in different structures, but what is important to notice is that there is always a way to turn that negative affirmation into a positive one. And that is the one you want to use to help you shift your thinking to a more life-supportive one.

The reason why you want to only use a positive context is:

1. It helps change your neuropathways in the brain.
2. The subconscious and conscious minds need to be in sync on the affirmation in order to manifest.
3. As you know, thoughts are things, so you want to think the good thoughts so you can manifest positive things in your life.
4. This is where the use of affirmations is so critical – they help you manifest what you want!

11

**More Examples of Negative Affirmations (So You Know What *Not* To Do!)**

- I waste less time on ineffective things at work.
- Money is no longer hard to earn.
- Wanting a romantic relationship is no longer a burden for me.
- My health stops deteriorating.

You got the picture......KEEP IT POSITIVE!

**A Benefit of Affirmations**

- Shift your negative patterns as, with practice, you become more aware of your thoughts, which allows less negativity to seep in

# Step 7
## Use the Present Tense and Give It a Time Frame

It is important to understand why you should use the present tense and preferably give a time frame by when something would be present in your life.

1.  The present tense tells your subconscious mind it is already happening, thus activating it into creating the things you are affirming. The time frame (the "by when" part of your affirmation) gets specific. It tells the subconscious that there is urgency, thus activating it to make sure the deadline is met.
2.  Please note: you must believe that it is possible! Remember Chapter 3; the affirmation has to be believable to you so it can be believable to your subconscious mind. So the deadline should be achievable and realistic.
3.  You don't have to give every affirmation a time frame. Time frames are used most with tangible goals (financial, weight loss, to name a few). Since affirmations must be followed up with actions, the time frame allows you to make sure you stay in action as you continue using the affirmation to empower and inspire you to keep going.
4.  An example of an affirmation in the present tense is: "Money flows easily and effortlessly to me."

## A Few Things to Remember

- Nothing is better than the present.
- Taking action in the present delivers results in the future.
- The future is brighter when intention is applied.

## A Few Things to Avoid

- Do not use "I *will*" in your affirmation; it puts the goal in the future and keeps it in the future.
- Do not use a date too far in the future; it will seem unattainable to you, thus not believable.
- Do not use "I am *going to*…" – it has the same effect of the future tense. It just keeps your goal in the unattainable future.

## A Benefit of Affirmations

- Help focus on your goals so you have more of what you want in your life

# Step 8
## Make It Personal and Take Action

This needs to be said again: Write your affirmations in the present tense; make them personal and positive and then take action!

Here is why:

1. When an affirmation is personal and hits your deepest core, it ignites a chain of reactions in the subconscious that is the bedrock of manifestation.
2. As you feel the connection to the affirmation, you must take appropriate action that is in alignment with whatever you are affirming.
3. For example, if your affirmation is around financial abundance, the action you might want to take is looking for a better paying job, starting your own business, applying for a loan to further your own business, creating a budget… something that would bring you more abundance. You must take proactive and positive steps that reinforce and support the affirmation you are using.
4. The subconscious mind will register this and keep collecting positive evidence and proof in favor of the affirmation and put the energetic wheels in motion that will result in your desired result.

**Exactly How Does It Work?**

- As you keep repeating your affirmations and taking action, you feel better – and as you feel better, your perspective shifts, and as your perspective shifts, your subconscious mind delivers what you want.

**A Benefit of Affirmations**

- Guide you to focus on positive thinking, thus helping you stay positive

# Step 9
## Add Power to Your Affirmation by Using a Comparative Adjective

A comparative is an adjective that compares nouns to one another. It is not obligatory to use comparatives, but they do make affirmations more fun and they are very helpful when you are working on something you feel you have a bigger block on.

There are three things to know about comparatives:

1. Comparatives can boost your affirmation because they give you a sense that you are working on something – it is all in process.
2. When using a comparative, you feel like there is no end to the goodness that the affirmation is bringing, so you are telling your subconscious to keep working on bringing you that which you are affirming.
3. Comparatives add substance and are just more fun!

For example, instead of saying "I make more money every day," say "I make more and more money every day." Repeat it every day, several times a day, in the shower, while exercising or while getting ready for bed, in order to stay grounded in the message.

## Examples of More Comparative Affirmations

- I lose more and more weight every day.
- I am feeling better by the minute.
- My business grows faster each month.

## A Benefit of Affirmations

- Help you keep the small things in perspective

# Step 10
## Write Your Affirmations!

Now you are ready to write your affirmation! You have learned that:

1. It is important to write your affirmation in the present tense.
2. It must be positive (not a positive negative).
3. It must be personal.
4. It must spark a feeling.
5. It must be believable to the subconscious mind.
6. Giving your affirmation a time frame is essential to making it powerful and realistic.
7. Using "I Am" and comparative verbs can help the subconscious mind and conscious mind get in sync with each other.
8. Taking action from your affirmation is just as important as saying your affirmation.

Go ahead and take some time and write an affirmation right now!

In the next chapter we will delve into what type of action is important for your affirmation to not only make you feel good, but to also generate the results you want.

## Questions to Keep You Focused As You Write Your Affirmations

- Am I writing about what is important to me?
- What do I really want to accomplish with this affirmation?
- Is it sparking a feeling in me when I read it?
- Do I believe that this affirmation will really help me?
- Is there anything else I need to add?

## A Benefit of Affirmations

- Help you hone in on your deepest desires

# Step 11
## Commitment, Dedication and Consistency

Once you have your affirmation(s) written down, the rubber meets the road! You must say your affirmation(s) every day, with feeling and gusto. On average, say 10-15 affirmations every day in the morning when you wake up and in the evening before you go to bed.

1. If you are a beginner, repeat your affirmations 3-5 times per day until you start feeling a shift in yourself from the affirmation. Repeat them as many times as you can to get the most out of them.
2. Be consistent! Saying them one day and then skipping a few days won't work! Discipline yourself in making them a part of your routine. Just like Yoga or meditation, make affirmations part of your daily life!
3. This is where commitment and dedication come into play. If you have a burning desire to change something in your life and shift your patterns and beliefs for the better, you will do whatever you need to do to make affirmations work for you.
4. Your life circumstances must not supersede your commitment to your affirmations. If you want your affirmations to work, you must not have any excuses! Just do it, and repeat them every day!

## Easy Steps to Help You Stay On Track

- Write your affirmations on flash cards.
- Keep them by your bed.
- Use an Affirmation Notebook with all your working affirmations in it.
- Update your affirmations when you feel you have received their benefit.
- Retire those you no longer need and write new ones.
- Use sticky notes on your bathroom mirror to remind yourself to say your affirmations.

## A Benefit of Affirmations

- Help you take action

# Step 12
## Affirmations 24/7

When you first start using affirmations, you want to really get into it. You want to write, read and say them often during the day so you get used to the process and used to hearing your voice saying those words you so lovingly and purposefully wrote. You won't have to do this forever, but at the beginning it is good to do to get yourself into the habit. By hearing your voice saying the empowering and positive messages, you are reprogramming the subconscious mind to the new beliefs and affirmations you are teaching it.

It is easy to forget, so creating a daily routine is key. This is how you can do this without it feeling like a burden:

1. Write each affirmation on a separate flash card you can take with you.
2. Decide which times are best for you to say them (i.e., in the morning as soon as you get up, after a meditation, on a break at work, before going to bed).
3. Use post-it notes to remind yourself.

If you forget, don't beat yourself up, just start again and move forward. Do what feels good to you, but always challenge yourself. Affirmations will work, if you put out the effort and intention to allowing them to shift your perceptions and limiting beliefs.

**Three Things to Take Note Of:**

When you feel you don't have time, or you are often forgetting to repeat your affirmations:

- Push yourself and make an effort to do your affirmations anyway.
- Get creative and change what is not working (maybe you need to change the time of day or frequency).
- Stay committed! Remember consistency is the key to optimum results.

You will thank yourself for it later!

## A Benefit of Affirmations

- Shift your perceptions of yourself that were taken on as a child, but that were not necessarily true, creating new, empowering self-perceptions that move you forward in life

# Step 13
## How Do I Know My Affirmations Are Working?

Just like an acorn takes up to 4 -5 weeks to sprout, so do affirmations. They say that it takes 90 days to form a habit and during that habit-forming period is when results start to show. There is always a gestation period and the more inner work you continue to do, the faster affirmations start working and the more potent they can be for your personal empowerment.

There are three things you can look for to know that your affirmations are working for you:

1. A renewed sense of hope and well-being. If your affirmations really touch you deeply, they will start making you feel good. Not only because you are now affirming a positive intention for your life, but also because you are deliberately reprogramming the subconscious mind for the better, empowering yourself in that new belief.
2. Your thoughts start leaning toward the positive more often in the area you are using the affirmations for. As you notice that positivity, you start feeling good about that area of life.
3. Your beliefs and thought patterns around the area you are working on are disappearing and your actions around that area are supportive of a positive change.

25

**Questions To Ask Yourself To Gauge Effectiveness:**

- "How do I feel today about the area of my life or belief that I am working on?" If your answer is better than the last one, you are making progress.
- "What is showing up in my life now that was not present before?" This question is designed to bring awareness to any energetic shifts happening because of the affirmations. If you notice new, positive or supporting events, people, situations and opportunities, then you are on the right track.
- "Who am I becoming? Am I becoming who I am intending?" These questions go hand-in-hand and bring awareness to any personality or character shifts that are happening as a result of saying your affirmations. If you feel stronger, more confident, self-assured, powerful, happy, relieved, hopeful around the area of life or belief you are working on, you are moving forward.
- "Do I feel complete with this affirmation?" If you feel closure in the area of life you have been using affirmations on, you have now graduated from that affirmation and it is time to move on to a new area with a new affirmation.

## A Benefit of Affirmations

- Help you notice synchronicities in your life that then motivate you to keep practicing and saying your affirmations daily

# Step 14
## Put Your Affirmations to the Test

Once you have the areas you want to work on, test your new affirmations out by saying them eight times per day the first five days you use them. This will help create consistency, ease you into a new habit and gauge if you are connected to the affirmation.

Yes, I know eight times a day seems like a lot, but checking into how you feel the first few days is imperative in understanding if the affirmation you wrote is emotionally-inspiring and provokes feelings, maximizing its effect.
This is how you can organize your first five days:

1. Before beginning, write down how you feel about the area of life or belief for which you wrote the affirmation.
2. Set an alarm every 2 hours, starting from the time you get up to the time you go to bed and say your affirmation every 2 hours (if you need to, go to the restroom or outside and say it so no one hears).
3. Take notes on how you feel before and after you say your affirmation, each time you say it (carry a small notepad for ease).
4. At the end of the five days, list all the positives you got from saying your affirmation in one column and compare them with what you wrote before starting your five-day affirmation test.

## An Important Note:

- Only you can really gauge if an affirmation is right for you and is working. The way to understand if it is, is to write how you feel around the area before and after you do your five-day affirmation test and read it back to see if you have more positive feelings than before you started using the affirmation.

## A Benefit of Affirmations

- Affirmations, custom written for you and by you, are uniquely designed to work for your personal benefit. This is why using previously written affirmations is not an effective way of using this process

# Step 15
## Sample Affirmations

Everyone will have their own unique way to write an affirmation and the more personal and detailed you make yours, the more the affirmation will work for you.

Last words:

1.  Keep in mind the sample affirmations below are very general, but could be used as a source of inspiration for those who are just starting out. Make sure you connect with them if you are going to use them or if you find any you like, you can make it your own by adding or deleting words.
2.  At first it might seem a bit silly, but keep going and keep deepening your connection with the affirmation as you continue to do your inner work.
3.  You will find that eventually you'll graduate from some of the sample affirmations and you will seek out new ones for your next level of expansion. It feels good to know that one area in your life has been resolved and you can move onto the next.
4.  Have fun and make empowering messages work for you, affirming and helping you manifest that which you want to see and have in your life!

## Finances:

- Money flows easily and effortlessly to me!
- Making money is easy!
- I make more and more money every day!
- I earn $10,000 per month as I offer my products and services and I enjoy the work I do by August 30th, 2017.
- Money helps people!

## Health:

- My body is healthy and strong!
- All my cells work together for maximum health!
- Every day I wake up feeling rested, energized and capable of doing anything!
- All my organs function together as they keep me strong, healthy and vibrant!
- My body is free to generate healthy cells and functions well to keep me going strong every day!

## Relationship:

- I am in a loving, committed, loyal, romantic relationship with a man by June 1st, 2017!
- My man loves, cares, respects and cherishes me!
- I wake up every day next to the man of my dreams and relish in the giddiness, joy and happiness I feel when I am with him.
- I am ready for a committed relationship now!
- My heart is full as I spend time with my beloved and I receive the love he gives me!

## Congratulations!

You have now finished learning how to write and use positive affirmations.

Please star rate this book.

Reviews are solid gold to writers. Please take a few minutes to give us some itty bitty feedback on this book.

## ABOUT THE AUTHOR

Micaela Passeri's mission is to empower women with self-confidence through positive messaging and positive thinking. One way she does this is through the clothing line and affirmations she designs and writes for Love You Revolution.

Micaela Passeri, born and raised in Florence Italy, is a Fashion Designer turned Confidence and Subconscious Mind expert. She is an author, speaker and the Co-President of the Santa Monica Holistic Chamber of Commerce. She specializes in experiential products, workshops and mentoring to help those on their soulful journey of self-discovery, self-confidence and self-love. Trained in NLP and Emotion Code, she creates profound shifts in life patterns and has helped hundreds of women love who they are; her most powerful tool – empowering messages, aka affirmations!

Micaela is committed to helping women empower themselves to see their true value, not only for those who can purchase her clothes and services and use them as empowerment tools, but also for those who cannot, so she brings her workshops, clothing line and transformative work to domestic violence shelters, LAUSD schools, YMCA, Boys & Girls Clubs and other non-profits at no cost.

Check out her clothing line and programs to help you reprogram your subconscious mind at:

www.LoveYouRevolution.com.

If You Enjoyed This Itty Bitty® Book You Might Also Enjoy…

- **Your Amazing Itty Bitty® Weight Loss Book –** Suzy Prudden and Joan Meijer-Hirschland

- **Your Amazing Itty Bitty® Self-Esteem Book –** Jade Elizabeth

- **Your Amazing Itty Bitty® Heal Your Body Book –** Patricia Garza Pinto

….and many more Itty Bitty® books available on line

Made in the USA
San Bernardino, CA
31 December 2019